WILDLIFE VIEWING AREAS

Tennessee Ecoregions

- Blue Ridge
- Ridge and Valley
- Southeastern Plains
- Interior Plateau
- Mississippi Valley Loess Plains
- Mississippi Alluvial Plain
- Southwestern Appalachians
- Central Appalachians

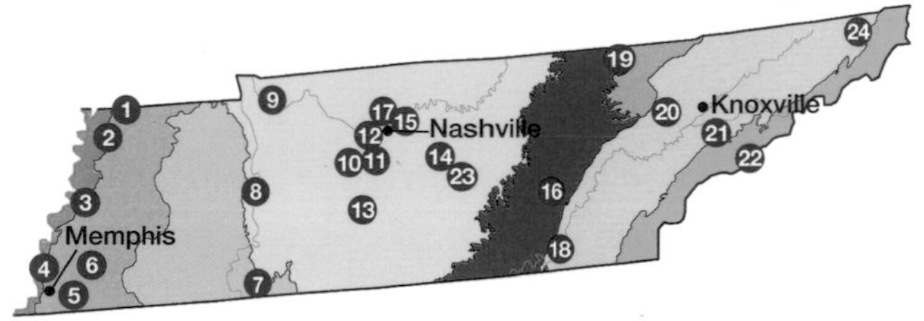

1. Reelfoot National Wildlife Refuge
2. Lake Isom National Wildlife Refuge
3. Chickasaw National Wildlife Refuge
4. Meeman-Shelby Forest State Park
5. Lichterman Nature Center
6. Hatchie National Wildlife Refuge
7. Pickwick Landing State Park
8. Tennessee National Wildlife Refuge
9. Cross Creeks National Wildlife Refuge
10. Bowie Nature Park
11. Owl's Hill Nature Sanctuary
12. Warner Park Nature Center
13. Tennessee Wildlife Observation Area Monsanto Ponds
14. Cedars of Lebanon State Park
15. Shelby Bottoms Nature Center
16. Fall Creek Falls State Park
17. Bells Bend Outdoor Center
18. Chattanooga Nature Center
19. Pickett State Park
20. University of Tennessee Arboretum
21. Ijams Nature Center
22. Great Smoky Mountains National Park
23. Discovery Center at Murfree Spring
24. Steele Creek Park & Nature Center

Most illustrations show the adult male in breeding coloration. Colors and markings may be duller or absent during different seasons. The measurements denote the length of animals from nose/bill to tail tip. Butterfly measurements denote wingspan. Illustrations are not to scale.

Waterford Press produces reference guides that introduce novices to nature, science, travel and languages. Product information is featured on the website: **www.waterfordpress.com**

Made in the USA

Text and illustrations © 2011, 2020 by Waterford Press Inc. All rights reserved. Cover images © Shutterstock. Ecoregion map © The National Atlas of the United States. To order, call 800-434-2555.
For permissions, or to share comments, e-mail editor@waterfordpress.com.
For information on custom-published products, call 800-434-2555 or e-mail info@waterfordpress.com.

ISBN 978-1-58355-630-6
$7.95 U.S.
UPC
10 9 8 7 6 5 4 3 2 1
205234

TENNESSEE WILDLIFE – A Folding Pocket Guide to Familiar Animals

Kavanagh/Leung

A POCKET NATURALIST® GUIDE

TENNESSEE WILDLIFE

A Folding Pocket Guide to Familiar Animals

INSECTS & INVERTEBRATES

Firefly
Photinus spp.
To 1.5 in. (4 cm)
Tennessee's state insect.

Cave Cricket
Ceuthophilus spp.
To 1 in. (3 cm)

Praying Mantis
Mantis religiosa
To 2.5 in. (6 cm)
Front legs are held as if praying.

Seven-spotted Lady Bug
Coccinella septempunctata
To .25 in. (.6 cm)
Tennessee's state insect.

Yellow Jacket
Vespula pensylvanica
To .63 in. (1.6 cm)
Aggressive picnic pest can sting repeatedly.

Honey Bee
Apis mellifera
To .75 in. (2 cm)
Slender bee has pollen baskets on its rear legs. Can only sting once.
Tennessee's state agricultural insect.

Cicada
Magicicada spp.
To 1.5 in. (4 cm)
Song is a sudden loud whine or buzz, maintained steadily before dying away.

Black Widow Spider
Latrodectus mactans
To .5 in. (1.3 cm)
Has red hourglass marking on abdomen. Venomous.

Chigger (Velvet Mite)
Family Trombidiidae
To .12 in. (.3 cm)
Tiny, biting woodland insects leave red welts on human skin.

Great Blue Skimmer
Libellula vibrans
To 2 in. (5 cm)
Like most dragonflies, it rests with its wings held open.

Black-and-yellow Garden Spider
Argiope aurantia
To 1.25 in. (3.2 cm)

Six-spotted Fishing Spider
Dolomedes triton
To .75 in. (2 cm)
Often seen running over floating vegetation.

True Katydid
Pterophylla camellifolia
To 2 in. (5 cm)
Loud 2-part call – *katy-DID* – is heard on summer evenings.

Twelve-spotted Skimmer
Libellula pulchella
To 2 in. (5 cm)
Each wing features black patches at the base, midpoint and tip.

Ebony Jewelwing
Calopteryx maculata
To 1.75 in. (4.5 cm)
Like most damselflies, it rests with its wings held together over its back.

BUTTERFLIES & MOTHS

Zebra Swallowtail
Eurytides marcellus
To 3.5 in. (9 cm)
Tennessee's state butterfly.

Eastern Tiger Swallowtail
Papilio glaucus
To 6 in. (15 cm)

Spicebush Swallowtail
Papilio troilus
To 4.5 in. (11 cm)
Note greenish hindwings.

Cabbage White
Pieris rapae
To 2 in. (5 cm)
One of the most common butterflies.

Mourning Cloak
Nymphalis antiopa
To 3.5 in. (9 cm)
Emerges during the first spring thaw.

Eastern Tailed Blue
Cupido comyntas
To 1 in. (3 cm)
Note orange spots above thread-like hindwing tails.

Red Admiral
Vanessa atalanta
To 2.5 in. (6 cm)

Long-tailed Skipper
Urbanus proteus
To 2 in. (5 cm)

Red-spotted Purple
Limenitis arthemis astyanax
To 3 in. (8 cm)

Buckeye
Junonia coenia
To 2.5 in. (6 cm)

Monarch
Danaus plexippus
To 4 in. (10 cm)

Viceroy
Limenitis archippus
To 3 in. (8 cm)
Told from similar monarch by its smaller size and the thin, black band on its hindwings.

Bumblebee Moth
Hemaris diffinis
To 2 in. (5 cm)
Distinguished by clear wings and furry body.

Appalachian Brown
Satyrodes appalachia
To 2 in. (5 cm)

Polyphemus Moth
Antheraea polyphemus
To 6 in. (15 cm)

Luna Moth
Actias luna
To 4.5 in. (11 cm)

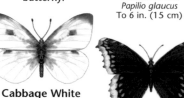

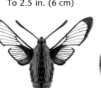

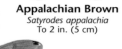

FISHES

Rainbow Trout
Oncorhynchus mykiss To 44 in. (1.1 m)
Note reddish side stripe.

Black Crappie
Pomoxis nigromaculatus
To 16 in. (40 cm)

Brown Trout
Salmo trutta To 40 in. (1 m)
Has red and black spots on its body.

Bluegill
Lepomis macrochirus
To 16 in. (40 cm)

Largemouth Bass
Micropterus salmoides To 40 in. (1 m)
Note prominent side spots.
Jaw joint extends past eye.
Tennessee's state sport fish.

Redear Sunfish
Lepomis microlophus
To 14 in. (35 cm)
Also called shellcracker.

Smallmouth Bass
Micropterus dolomieu To 27 in. (68 cm)
Jaw joint is beneath the eye.
Tennessee's second state sport fish.

Hybrid Bass
Morone hybrid To 20 in. (50 cm)
Note broken side stripes.
Striped and white bass hybrid is an aggressive sport fish.

Striped Bass
Morone saxatilis To 6 ft. (1.8 m)
Has 6-9 dark side stripes.

Common Carp
Cyprinus carpio To 30 in. (75 cm)
Introduced species has an arched back and mouth barbels.

Flathead Catfish
Pylodictis olivaris To 5 ft. (1.5 m)
Head is long and flat. Upper lobe of caudal fin is white.

Channel Catfish
Ictalurus punctatus
To 4 ft. (1.2 m)
Note adipose fin, black-spotted sides and rounded anal fin.
Tennessee's state commercial fish.

Yellow Bullhead
Ameiurus natalis To 18 in. (45 cm)
Chin barbels are white or yellow.

REPTILES & AMPHIBIANS

Tennessee Cave Salamander
Gyrinophilus palleucus To 9 in. (23 cm)
Note external gills. **Tennessee's state amphibian.**

Red Eft
Notophthalmus viridescens
To 6 in. (15 cm)
Juvenile form of a red-spotted newt.

American Toad
Anaxyrus americanus
To 4.5 in. (11 cm)
Call is a high musical trill lasting up to 30 seconds.

Bullfrog
Lithobates catesbeianus
To 8 in. (20 cm)
Call is a deep-pitched – *jurrrooom.*

Crawfish Frog
Lithobates areolata
To 4.5 in. (11 cm)
Call is deep, resonating snore.

Five-lined Skink
Plestiodon fasciatus
To 8 in. (20 cm)
Has 5 light dorsal stripes.

Snapping Turtle
Chelydra serpentina To 18 in. (45 cm)
Note knobby shell and long tail.

Eastern Box Turtle
Terrapene carolina
To 9 in. (23 cm)
Note high-domed shell.
Tennessee's state reptile.

Scarlet Snake
Cemophora coccinea To 32 in. (80 cm)
Color bands do not encircle body.

Corn Snake
Pantherophis guttatus
To 6 ft. (1.8 m)
Told by black-bordered red blotches.

Timber Rattlesnake
Crotalus horridus To 6 ft. (1.8 m)
Note black tail.

Eastern Rat Snake
Elaphe obsoleta
To 8 ft. (2.4 m)

Northern Water Snake
Nerodia sipedon To 4.5 ft. (1.4 m)
Note dark blotches on back.

Copperhead
Agkistrodon contortrix To 52 in. (1.3 m)
Venomous snake has hourglass-shaped bands down its back.

Cottonmouth
Agkistrodon piscivorus To 6 ft. (1.8 m)
Large, venomous water snake has a spade-shaped head.

Canada Goose
Branta canadensis
To 45 in. (1.14 m)

Northern Pintail
Anas acuta To 30 in. (75 cm)

Wood Duck
Aix sponsa To 20 in. (50 cm)

Mallard
Anas platyrhynchos
To 28 in. (70 cm)

Green-winged Teal
Anas crecca To 16 in. (40 cm)

Great Blue Heron
Ardea herodias
To 4.5 ft. (1.4 m)

Black-crowned Night-Heron
Nycticorax nycticorax
To 28 in. (70 cm)

Great Egret
Ardea alba
To 38 in. (95 cm)
Note yellow bill
and black feet.

Ring-billed Gull
Larus delawarensis
To 20 in. (50 cm)
Bill has dark ring.

Herring Gull
Larus argentatus
To 26 in. (65 cm)
Legs are pinkish.

Killdeer
Charadrius vociferus
To 12 in. (30 cm)
Note two breast bands.

American Coot
Fulica americana
To 16 in. (40 cm)

Ruby-throated Hummingbird
Archilochus colubris
To 3.5 in. (9 cm)

Northern Bobwhite
Colinus virginianus
To 12 in. (30 cm)
Tennessee's state
game bird.

Wild Turkey
Meleagris gallopavo
To 4 ft. (1.2 m)

Mourning Dove
Zenaida macroura
To 13 in. (33 cm)
Call is a mournful –
oooh-woo-woo-woo.

Yellow-billed Cuckoo
Coccyzus americanus
To 14 in. (35 cm)

Belted Kingfisher
Megaceryle alcyon
To 14 in. (35 cm)

Rock Pigeon
Columba livia
To 13 in. (33 cm)

Red-headed Woodpecker
Melanerpes erythrocephalus
To 10 in. (25 cm)

Hairy Woodpecker
Dryobates villosus
To 10 in. (25 cm)
The similar downy
woodpecker is
smaller and has a
shorter bill.

Pileated Woodpecker
Dryocopus pileatus
To 17 in. (43 cm)
Note large size.

Carolina Wren
Thryothorus ludovicianus
To 6 in. (15 cm)

Tree Swallow
Tachycineta bicolor
To 6 in. (15 cm)

Purple Martin
Progne subis
To 8 in. (20 cm)

White-breasted Nuthatch
Sitta carolinensis
To 6 in. (15 cm)

Loggerhead Shrike
Lanius ludovicianus
To 9 in. (23 cm)
Note hooked bill
and black mask.

Turkey Vulture
Cathartes aura
To 32 in. (80 cm)
Note red head.

Red-tailed Hawk
Buteo jamaicensis
To 25 in. (63 cm)

Bald Eagle
Haliaeetus leucocephalus
To 40 in. (1 m)

Sharp-shinned Hawk
Accipiter striatus
To 14 in. (35 cm)
Note square-edged tail
and striped breast.

Cooper's Hawk
Accipiter cooperii
To 20 in. (50 cm)
Note long, rounded
white-tipped tail.
Often found in
urban areas.

Barred Owl
Strix varia
To 2 ft. (60 cm)
Call is a loud –
who-cooks-for-you?
who-cooks-for-
you-all?

Black Vulture
Coragyps atratus
To 27 in. (68 cm)
Note gray wing tips.

Gray Catbird
Dumetella carolinensis
To 9 in. (23 cm)
Note black cap. Call has
cat-like 'mew' notes.

American Robin
Turdus migratorius
To 11 in. (28 cm)

Eastern Bluebird
Sialia sialis
To 7 in. (18 cm)

European Starling
Sturnus vulgaris
To 8 in. (20 cm)

Red-winged Blackbird
Agelaius phoeniceus
To 9 in. (23 cm)

Common Grackle
Quiscalus quiscula
To 14 in. (35 cm)

Tufted Titmouse
Baeolophus bicolor
To 6 in. (15 cm)

Carolina Chickadee
Poecile carolinensis
To 4.5 in. (11 cm)
Song is a name-saying –
chickadee-dee-dee.

Dark-eyed Junco
Junco hyemalis
To 7 in. (18 cm)

American Crow
Corvus brachyrhynchos
To 22 in. (55 cm)

Northern Mockingbird
Mimus polyglottos
To 11 in. (28 cm)
Tennessee's
state bird.

Eastern Meadowlark
Sturnella magna
To 9 in. (23 cm)

Northern Cardinal
Cardinalis cardinalis
To 9 in. (23 cm)

Blue Jay
Cyanocitta cristata
To 14 in. (35 cm)

House Sparrow
Passer domesticus
To 6 in. (15 cm)

Common Yellowthroat
Geothlypis trichas
To 5 in. (13 cm)

Yellow-rumped Warbler
Setophaga coronata
To 6 in. (15 cm)

Rose-breasted Grosbeak
Pheucticus ludovicianus
To 9 in. (23 cm)

Baltimore Oriole
Icterus galbula
To 8 in. (20 cm)

Scarlet Tanager
Piranga olivacea
To 7 in. (18 cm)

Indigo Bunting
Passerina cyanea
To 6 in. (15 cm)

House Finch
Haemorhous mexicanus
To 6 in. (15 cm)

American Goldfinch
Spinus tristis
To 5 in. (13 cm)

Virginia Opossum
Didelphis virginiana
To 40 in. (1 m)
Note long fur
and naked tail.

Big Brown Bat
Eptesicus fuscus
To 5 in. (13 cm)

Eastern Cottontail
Sylvilagus floridanus
To 18 in. (45 cm)

Eastern Gray Squirrel
Sciurus carolinensis
To 20 in. (50 cm)

Woodchuck
Marmota monax
To 32 in. (80 cm)

Swamp Rabbit
Sylvilagus aquaticus
To 22 in. (55 cm)

White-footed Mouse
Peromyscus leucopus
To 8 in. (20 cm)
Distinguished by its white
undersides and hairy tail.

Norway Rat
Rattus norvegicus
To 18 in. (45 cm)
Brown to gray rodent
has a naked tail.

Fox Squirrel
Sciurus niger
To 28 in. (70 cm)
Note large size and bushy
tail. Coat may be red-
brown, gray or black.

Eastern Woodrat
Neotoma floridana
To 16 in. (40 cm)

Common Muskrat
Ondatra zibethicus
To 2 ft. (60 cm)
Aquatic rodent has a naked tail
that is flattened on its sides.

American Beaver
Castor canadensis
To 4 ft. (1.2 m)

Nutria
Myocastor coypus To 56 in. (1.4 m)
Introduced aquatic rodent
has become a serious pest.

Nine-banded Armadillo
Dasypus novemcinctus
To 32 in. (80 cm)
Found in W. Tennessee.

Common Raccoon
Procyon lotor To 40 in. (1 m)
Tennessee's state wild animal.

Striped Skunk
Mephitis mephitis
To 32 in. (80 cm)

Mink
Neovison vison
To 28 in. (70 cm)
Chin is white.

Bobcat
Lynx rufus
To 4 ft. (1.2 m)

Northern River Otter
Lontra canadensis
To 52 in. (1.3 m)

Common Gray Fox
Urocyon cinereoargenteus
To 3.5 ft. (1.1 m)
Note black-tipped tail.

Red Fox
Vulpes vulpes To 40 in. (1 m)
Note white-tipped tail.

Wild Hog
Sus scrofa To 6 ft. (1.8 m)
Introduced species is descended
from the Eurasian wild boar.

Coyote
Canis latrans To 52 in. (1.3 m)

Black Bear
Ursus americanus
To 6 ft. (1.8 m)

White-tailed Deer
Odocoileus virginianus
To 7 ft. (2.1 m)